Well-Being

BALBOA.
PRESS

A DIVISION OF HAY HOUSE

Balboa Press books may be ordered through booksellers or by contacting:

Balboa Press
A Division of Hay House
1663 Liberty Drive
Bloomington, IN 47403
www.balboapress.com
1 (877) 407-4847

Because of the dynamic nature of the Internet, any web addresses or links contained in
this book may have changed since publication and may no longer be valid. The views
expressed in this work are solely those of the author and do not necessarily reflect the
views of the publisher, and the publisher hereby disclaims any responsibility for them.

The author of this book does not dispense medical advice or prescribe the use of any
technique as a form of treatment for physical, emotional, or medical problems without the
advice of a physician, either directly or indirectly. The intent of the author is only to offer
information of a general nature to help you in your quest for emotional and spiritual well-
being. In the event you use any of the information in this book for yourself, which is your
constitutional right, the author and the publisher assume no responsibility for your actions.

Any people depicted in stock imagery provided by Getty Images are models,
and such images are being used for illustrative purposes only.
Certain stock imagery © Getty Images.

Print information available on the last page.

ISBN: 978-1-5043-9881-7 (sc)
ISBN: 978-1-5043-9882-4 (e)

Balboa Press rev. date: 02/21/2018

Table of Contents

Preface vii

Part 1 Teaching
    Chapter 1   Need...3
    Chapter 2   Value 5
    Chapter 3   Object 7
    Chapter 4   Subject 9
    Chapter 5   Ignorance 11
    Chapter 6   Knowledge 13
    Chapter 7   Experience 16
    Chapter 8   Health 19
    Chapter 9   Identity 22

Part 2 Sources
    Chapter 10 Psychology..27
    Chapter 11 Spirituality..31
    Chapter 12 Philosophy...38
    Chapter 13 Theology 43
    Chapter 14 Shakti..47
    Chapter 15 Nonduality 54
    Chapter 16 Conclusion 58

Coda 65
Bibliography...67
About The Author...69

Preface

The purpose of this book is to present several simple yet fundamental principles I have learned over the last fifty years of working to improve my own mental health and well being. The book is divided into two parts: teaching and sources. The first part, teaching, will be short and its style lean, primarily to facilitate easy reading and absorption of the material. The second part, sources, will be more academic in style yet still relatively lean, intended for those interested in the source material for the teaching portion of the book. The first part of the book may be read by itself without reading the second part for anyone primarily interested in a very short, very direct account of the principles of the teaching.

In the first, teaching part of the book I will also be directly addressing the reader as if we were face to face in private conversation. As a way of making the reader more comfortable I should write a few words about my own background.

Both my education and professional life have been varied, yet both have contributed to the understanding presented in this book. I have education and experience in business, psychology, religious studies, philosophy, theology, social work, teaching, library science, world and English literature, hospital and hospice chaplaincy, and addiction counseling. My current employment is as a hospice chaplain. All of this experience may suggest either aimless wandering or an inability to settle into one career or profession. Yet the truth is that I have always wanted as broad a perspective as possible, partly as a way to help myself and others attain a better quality of life. As far as a professional life is concerned, I have settled into hospice chaplaincy, into which I pour all my knowledge and experience to improve the quality of life for dying patients and their families.

At the same time, however, what I have to offer as a chaplain is, due to time and opportunity constraints, limited to presence, comfort, and support, with little time available to present in an orderly fashion the principles I will share in this book.

I am also a seasoned writer, and have presented many of these principles before in a trilogy, written in an academic style: *Invicti Solis*, *The Liberation of Thought*, and *The Sickness of Effort*. I then followed this trilogy with a fourth book, *Role Playing*. Although these books are available and helpful, a more scholarly, academic approach to writing is not congenial to many readers. Hence this book, intended to reach a wider audience.

In the world of spirituality I have over fifty years experience seeking answers to questions about ultimate concern and meaning, and thirty of those years in an organized spiritual tradition. After I had attained a sufficient level of understanding in that one tradition, I began a serious exploration of several other traditions as well, in personal encounters with teachers and organized groups.

Enough about me. This book is about you, the reader. Thank you for reading this far. My hope is that reading further will make a difference in your life, in your ability to access your own innate well being.

PART ONE

Teaching

CHAPTER ONE

Need

Many self-help and even spiritual books begin by asking readers what they want. I am asking you to ponder the question more deeply: what do you need?

You should know what you want, of course. But you should also be able to distinguish what you want from what you need. You may want an expensive car or home, but do you really need them? What you actually need is transportation and shelter, and to meet those needs you don't have to extend yourself or your pocketbook beyond a certain extent.

Now whether you decide to invest more money in more expensive items is your choice. What is important, and what is important about the principle of need, is that you understand that what you may want is not necessarily what you actually need.

I would now like to discuss with you the word *desire*. Desire is often used as a synonym for the word *want*. I may want or desire a piece of pie, but what I really need is nourishment, provided I am actually hungry. In this case the desire for pie is a rather distant and somewhat distorted expression or reflection of the need for nourishment. If I reflect upon that desire I can see that it distorts the need for food by suggesting to me that what I need is a specific sort of food, and a high calorie one at that. The desire also tends to distract me from the need to make responsible choices in what I eat, taking into consideration my health, weight, and physical condition. In addition, the desire also distances me from the real fulfillment of the need, nourishment, and replaces it with another, pleasure. What I want or desire is not the nourishment of my physical body at all but the pleasure of eating; pleasure has become an end in itself, thus both distancing me from the conscious realization of my need and distorting it through replacing its intended end with another.

Again, if what you want or desire is a piece of pie, fine; it's your choice. But you need to be clear about the principle of need and how real need can be frustrated by desire. In the case of hunger, you feel a desire for food which is a faithful reflection of the need for nourishment. You are then clear about your options, whether you want to eat a balanced meal or indulge in some tasty treat that may or may not supply the needed nutrients.

Why, you may ask, is all this important? It is important because we all feel the need for something more; we feel that something is lacking; we feel a sense of privation. And the principle of need states that a felt need – which is desire – cannot arise unless there is some possibility of meeting that need, some "thing" that we lack, that we don't have, that we need to seek and find.

Some people are gifted enough and lucky enough to obtain what they think they need, only to find that it's not enough. No matter how much they may obtain, no matter how many triumphs or successes, they still feel empty, unfulfilled; they still have a felt need for more. But more of what? More money, more sexual conquests, more cars, homes, positions of power? Such people will tell you that what they have is never enough. They are unfulfilled; they are still seeking.

Some of these people are confused by desire. Unable to distinguish between different qualities of desire, between faithful and unfaithful reflections of need, they persist in the mistaken idea that pursuing what they want will inevitably bring them happiness or fulfillment. But an unfaithful reflection of need will always fall far short of the mark; at most its fulfillment will yield only a temporary feeling of satisfaction, soon to be forgotten and replaced by yet another desire.

You may be one of those. Or you may be one of the larger number of people who have not been able to obtain many of the desired objects in your life. Regardless, it is important to keep in mind the distinction between need and desire, and furthermore how normal it is to *value* what you think will meet your needs.

CHAPTER TWO

Value

I don't want to wax academic about value with you. It would be easy to do that because whole libraries can be filled with books about the topic of value. Instead I want us to ponder value as it relates to need.

Consider for yourself: don't you value what you think will meet your needs? Value simply means importance, what is important. If you think a particular object or person will meet your needs, that object or person will become important to you; you will value it.

Let's say you want to enter a particular profession, for example being a doctor. Whatever it takes to attain that objective, whatever education or experience you need, will be important to you. You may like or dislike your classroom education; you may like or dislike your intern or residency training, yet through it all you will value these experiences as necessary hurdles to obtain your degree and become a practicing physician. If your wish or desire is strong enough you will be able to overcome all difficulties in order to attain your objective.

Yet consider also: is the desire to become a doctor really a faithful reflection of a real need? Do you really need to be a doctor, or is the need rather for meaningful work, what the Buddhists call "right livelihood"? After becoming clearer about your real need you still wish to fulfill that need through becoming a doctor, you at least understand that your chosen profession is only one among many options you could choose to fulfill a need for meaningful work.

You can now see why I began with the distinction between need and desire before talking about value. It is important for you to be clear about this distinction before jumping to valuation. For a premature valuation may not only blind you to other avenues of fulfillment but also distort the actual need by distancing you from its possible satisfaction. You may find that being a doctor is not for you at all; while that unpleasant discovery may occur at any point along your journey, a better understanding of the originating need will allow you to adapt to changing feelings more readily as you contemplate other options of fulfillment. You will be able to see, perhaps in opposition to family and friends, that the desire to be a doctor was a rather distant reflection of the need for a meaningful career. Attaching valuation to one option only will make unpleasant transitions all the more painful.

The principle of value or valuation simply states that we value whatever we *think* will meet our needs. It is therefore even more important to be clear about the distinction between need and desire. It is important that we value faithful reflections of need rather than unfaithful reflections. And you should also know that this discrimination applies also to those objects that purport to satisfy or fulfill us.

CHAPTER THREE

Object

We are told by family, friends, teachers, and the culture at large, that in order to satisfy needs or desires we have to obtain objects. If we want to satisfy hunger we have to obtain food; if we want to satisfy a need for companionship we have to obtain companions or at least one companion; if we want a meaningful career we have to choose among career options. And so on.

An object, defined here, is any outside thing, entity, or person that will fulfill or meet a need or desire. By *outside* I mean outside ourselves. In the world as it appears to us, I am the subject here, you are the object there. That does not mean I am free to *treat* you as an object; it only means that from my point of view I am a subject, everything outside me is an object.

The three examples given in the first paragraph – the obtaining of food, companionship, and career – are legitimate cases of objects fulfilling particular needs or desires. If I want a companion then only a companion will meet that need, and the desire for companionship is a faithful reflection of that need. So when the companion is obtained, the need is met.

Yet what so often happens, in the case of companionship, is that the companion is expected to meet *all* our needs. Perhaps you have experienced this phenomenon: you wish for someone who will not only meet your need for a companion but also meet ever so many other needs as well. When your companion inevitably falls short of this expectation, disappointment and disillusionment set in, sometimes leading to the undermining of the relationship. The relationship dissolves and the search begins again for another companion, one who *this* time will fulfill our other needs. After several failed attempts you may decide to give up on relationships and perhaps turn to other avenues of fulfillment, some of which are detrimental and even destructive.

What has happened is that a desire so distant from the originating need has completely distorted the actual possibility of fulfillment by introducing unrealistic expectations of satisfaction into what originally was meant to fulfill one specific need.

Or perhaps you believe that becoming a doctor will fulfill all need for meaning, for a meaningful life. The originating need was for a meaningful career, but the desire changes that into a futile attempt to find meaning itself in one's profession. While that attempt may last for a time, it is bound to fall short as you age and your professional skill sets tend to diminish along with physical and psychological acuity.

Others try to find lasting fulfillment through a combination of met needs: career, family, religion, friends, activities, and so on. Again, if you are lucky enough to establish all these satisfactions, they will not suffice to bring permanent happiness or fulfillment. Why not?

Because they do not last; they and all objects are subject to change. That is the nature of objects: they can meet real need when precisely targeted and only for a time, but they cannot deliver lasting satisfaction or happiness. They change, and so do we. You and I change too, and between our changes and the changes inherent in any object the satisfaction we once felt is bound to erode.

It is also important for you to understand that family, friends, teachers, and the culture at large are all mistaken regarding the *source* or *cause* of our happiness or satisfaction. The culture conditions us to believe that the source or cause of our happiness is in the obtaining of objects. But the truth is quite otherwise: the source is in the subject.

CHAPTER FOUR

Subject

The source or cause of your happiness or satisfaction is not in any object; the source is you.

Why, then, does it appear that the source or cause of satisfaction is in the object, and why does the culture at large overlook the subject?

It is a natural and understandable mistake to make. When you desire something or someone very much and you obtain that thing or one, the desire vanishes and happiness floods the heart. What is the source of that happiness? You, not the object.

Yet it *appears* to be an object because every time a desired object is obtained the satisfaction or happiness also obtains. You and I need to ponder this phenomenon.

We will not consider the question of a default mental health state in depth until a future chapter, yet it needs to be mentioned here. Authentic psychology, and spiritual teachings, maintain that beneath all the desires for this and that object lies a default state of health and well being. It is actually not a "state" but the true nature of you, me, every human being. We will explore this matter further farther on in the book; for now treat it as a working hypothesis in considering the question of the true source of satisfaction and happiness.

Now consider the source of dissatisfaction and unhappiness: desire. It is desire that makes us dissatisfied, unhappy, and we are led to believe that obtaining an object will bring lasting satisfaction, lasting happiness. You and I know from experience that *lasting* satisfaction does not come from obtaining any object; in fact, you may even feel that lasting satisfaction is a chimera, an unfulfillable dream. You may have come to see that the promise of lasting happiness cannot obtain from the possession of any object. And that it has something to do with change: that you change and that objects also change. What is wanted or needed, apparently, is a source of happiness that does not change.

So our agitation, our dissatisfaction, our unhappiness, comes from desire, unfulfilled desire, whether we are new to life or have grown old trying to obtain lasting satisfaction. And when we do succeed in fulfilling a desire, the agitation vanishes and the true source of happiness appears. What you must see, what you must understand, is that the source of your happiness, your satisfaction, is always already available, waiting to fill and bless you, only veiled from your experience by the constant arising of one desire after another, and veiled also by the mistaken belief that happiness resides in the obtaining of objects.

You are the source of happiness, and what prevents your accessing this source in your consistent experience is a lack of knowledge; what prevents the more consistent appearance of this experience is ignorance.

CHAPTER FIVE

Ignorance

Authentic psychology and spiritual teachings are in agreement that the subject – we ourselves, you and I – is the source of our well being, our happiness and fulfillment. In its ignorance of this fact the culture teaches that we must obtain objects to find any possible fulfillment in life.

Ignorance here does not mean primarily lacking intellectual information but rather *ignoring* the essential part of ourselves, our true nature. We are taught to pay attention to what is "up front," to what appears to be our makeup, our conditioning or personality, and in so doing ignore what is deeper, what is veiled behind all the thoughts and feelings that serve the process of desire.

By *process of desire* I am not only referring to specific desires for this or that object; I am referring to a process of identifying ourselves with the operation of desire itself. An impulse arises in ourselves to satisfy a particular need; in identifying with that impulse we create a desire that may or may not be a faithful reflection of a real need. The intelligence of my true nature can only be reflected clearly in a quiet mind; when your mind is agitated by desire that intelligence, that source of well being, is veiled, unable to make itself felt – until, that is, the desire is removed and so the agitation is removed. The mind, relieved of the pressure of the desire, is able to quiet, become clear, and reflect the peace and well being of the self, our true nature. But because we have been taught that the source of well being is in an object, we necessarily *ignore* what happens to us and in so doing fail to follow the source of that well being inside, to inquire into our self, our true nature.

All of this may seem overwhelming to you, and I understand your feeling; I have felt it myself. But if you will persist, continue in dialogue with me, treat it all as a working hypothesis only, I assure you it will become clearer as we proceed.

If it is true that you and I and the holding culture have been victims of ignorance, it follows that what you and I most need is knowledge.

CHAPTER SIX

Knowledge

You and I have been victims of ignorance, but our spiritual traditions offer knowledge as a cure. This knowledge is always presented in such a way that it can be validated by experience, but that we will cover in the next chapter. For now, we will explore the knowledge in ideas, inevitably intellectual at first.

The ancient teaching is that you have two natures, one that changes and one changeless, one that is acquired over time and one that is timeless. The nature that is subject to time and change is the more noticeable part, the part that our culture notices more and that highlights all the time, from the moment we are made members of a family until we die. Psychology refers to it as our conditioning or personality, and it is subject to modification, to change. It is more noticeable, and it receives more notice, because of the process of desire.

Almost all our conditioning, almost all our thoughts and feelings, are in service to this process. The agitation, the dissatisfaction, we feel in the desiring process motivates us to give attention to whatever object we think will bring this state of agitation to an end. Yet in this attention is a clue to our changeless nature, our true self.

Consider: if you examine your inner life, which is deeper, your thoughts and emotions, or your awareness of them? Is it not your awareness? You are aware of thoughts, for example. Which is more fundamental, more essential, the awareness or the thoughts? If you remove the thoughts, what remains? The awareness, the attention. If you remove awareness, what remains? Nothing, for without awareness there could be no thought to notice. Awareness or attention is deeper, more essential than psychic objects like thoughts and feelings.

Awareness is your true nature.

You can validate this idea now. At this moment, of what are you aware? Of this paper, or the words on this paper? A thought or a feeling? Whatever you are aware of, that is an object in your experience; it is an object of your awareness.

Recall that we discussed subject and object in previous chapters. You are the subject, everything outside you is an object. Equally important is the understanding that you, the subject, are awareness, while everything seen by awareness is an object, whether it is a physical object or a subtle object like a thought, feeling, or sensation. Whatever you are aware *of* is an object; you, the subject, awareness, are the seer of those objects. And you also remember that the source of happiness or satisfaction is the subject, not the object.

What this means is that you are not your conditioning, not your beliefs, your thoughts, your emotions, your bodily sensations; what you are is awareness, attention. Attention is your response to life and your responsibility. You can choose to place your attention on this or that object, and you are responsible for where you place it. Attention can be directed toward the outside, toward objects, toward thoughts, feelings, and sensations in the mistaken belief that they are you, or it can be directed deeper, more inward, toward a recognition of the awareness that you always already are.

Remember that the process of desire is a process of identification; when you believe that you are your objects of experience you identify *yourself* with those objects. The end result of that identification is a mind full of agitation, always disturbed by an endless procession of desires, the satisfaction of which provides a brief glimpse of your source of well being but is overlooked, ignored as the true source of your *identity*, your very self, your true nature, your changeless, timeless being.

The principle of knowledge does not say that you will obtain the sort of knowledge you obtain in school; it is not a subject knowing an object. Authentic knowledge does not remove the mystery of life or of our being; it does not make all things known, nor does it touch the unknown in such a way as to clear up all mystery. It is rather a knowing that is being, an understanding that comes from recognizing the fact of being itself. I know that I am awareness not because I "know" awareness as a subject knows an object, as a student in school knows an object of study, but rather because I *am* awareness. I *do* need to be taught this fact, because my ignorance of my true nature cannot be removed without a teaching, but once I am properly prepared, properly taught, I can assimilate the teaching and by so doing come to understand my being simply because awareness is my nature. Just the thought that I am awareness takes me immediately to its reflection in the mind.

Knowledge, the principle of knowledge, is the corrective to your ignorance, to culture's consistent overlooking of the true source of culture itself. You should also know that this knowledge can help you understand the significance of your experience.

CHAPTER SEVEN

Experience

The knowledge taught by spirituality and authentic psychology maintains that your true nature is awareness, timeless and changeless, that it is senior to all contents of consciousness, all thoughts, emotions, and sensations, senior to all experiences whatsoever, and because of that seniority is capable of validating your experience, allowing you to interpret correctly the discrete experiences of your real self.

Understand: your true nature, awareness itself, is beyond experience. It is senior to experience and so experience cannot know it as a subject knows an object. Awareness can never be an object of experience because it is the Subject; it cannot be seen as an object of experience is seen; it is the One doing the seeing.

Yet it can be reflected clearly, and so experienced *as* a clear reflection, in a quiet mind. It is always reflected in the mind, but in an agitated mind it is much harder to detect as a discrete experience, one that can communicate its reality to the mind. And that is the chief impediment to discovering the reality of your well being: a mind agitated by desire. Without the needed knowledge an agitated mind makes it almost impossible to *experience* discrete features of reflected awareness like peace, joy, love, compassion, happiness, contentment or satisfaction, lasting fulfillment, and, deeper yet, the silence of stillness and a different circulation of energy.

The function of knowledge is not to add additional information to an already stuffed and overloaded mind; its function is to clear the mind of its stuffing, to make more likely the *discovery* of well being as well as the *development* of the ability to return again and again to this source. Accepting, for now, the truth of this knowledge, you can actually become more sensitive to those moments when desire is temporarily sated, the mind clears of agitation, and the well being of the real self or identity emerges from behind the veil of mental disturbance.

Once the discovery is made, you can then become more interested in the additional truths contained in this universal body of knowledge, truths like the changeless, timeless nature of your real self, its seniority to all contents of the mind, and its always already availability as the source of well being.

What this means is that you don't have to wait for a desire to be sated to experience well being. You can turn to it, turn within, whenever you wish, remembering that *you are responsible for where you place your attention*. Will you place your attention on the process of desire with its agitation and dissatisfaction, or will you seek within for your source of well being? It is up to you.

With enough experience you will begin to see that well being is your default. Previously you may have thought it was in your motivation to attain whatever desire was uppermost in your mind, a constant arising and satisfying of desire. Now you begin to see that your default is well being itself, not a *state* of well being but a changeless well being that is always experienced in the mind as a faithful reflection of awareness itself, of your true nature.

You must understand that states of mind come and go, experiences come and go; they all arise and pass away. But awareness does not come and go; it is always already present. Without changeless awareness there would be no experience at all; awareness is the substance as well as the container of experience; without it we would not be conscious at all; without it we would not be.

Because well being is your very nature, it is not a state that can arise and pass away. It can, however, be veiled by ignorance, by a mistaken use of your attention to notice only the more surface phenomena of awareness and ignore the deeper springs within.

What is missing is not only the discrete experience of the self but also the knowledge needed to understand the import of such experience. What we lack, the privation we feel, is the lack of a combination of discrete experiences and knowledge or understanding. Not subject-object knowledge, but a kind of knowing that can reveal the truth of spiritual, psychological knowledge experientially. For once this truth is experienced, validated and understood through knowledge, we have the potential to access our well being any time we wish. And it is this potential, this access, that can yield lasting mental health for you.

It is important to understand that experience does not validate knowledge, knowledge validates experience. You can have any number of discrete experiences of your true nature and without knowledge be unable to understand their true import. This fact was true in my own case. I had years of consistent, discrete self experiences before obtaining the knowledge needed to interpret them correctly, to understand their significance. Experience cannot remove ignorance, only knowledge can. With the right combination of experience and knowledge lasting mental, emotional, and spiritual health can be yours.

CHAPTER EIGHT

Health

Health is certainly an important feature of human existence, and no doubt you have returned to this topic frequently during the course of your life. It is natural to seek help from professionals whenever we feel our health is in question. But while most of us have little doubt who to consult when our physical well being is threatened, much confusion and doubt has obtained when our mental health is involved.

You may have encountered such feelings of doubt over the years. Most of this confusion is due to a confusion of tongues in the mental health field. I will not bore you with a detailed recounting of this confusion, though I will need to provide a couple of examples later in this chapter to illustrate the phenomenon; suffice it to say that those psychological approaches and treatments that do not comport well with spiritual teaching have limited – though sometimes beneficial – ability to challenge ignorance, while those psychological ideas and methods that do comport well with spiritual teachings can have far more beneficial effects in affecting lasting mental health.

Truth is truth, knowledge is knowledge, and whether it comes packaged as a spiritual or a psychological teaching matters little so long as it is presented in such a way first to connect with your immediate and common experience and second help lead you to a more complete experience of your real identity. The knowledge I have presented to you thus far is intended to accomplish those two steps toward deeper access to your well being, your default setting.

The mental health field has for too long been interested not in health but in sickness, in brokenness, in lostness. Of course this interest was intended to heal, but the focus of attention remained in the field of privation, not the field of fullness and completeness. Clinicians were taught to abide in the former field, and in turn taught their clients to abide there. Efforts were directed to correct errors in behavior and cognition without a radical redirection of attention toward the authentic source of mental health.

Take the case of a man caught in a continual round of dysfunctional thinking about his self-worth. His lack of self regard is continually reinforced by negative thoughts about himself. The clinician or therapist treating this fellow might prescribe exercises to make him more aware of his unhelpful thoughts and strongly suggest that he challenge those ideas, perhaps substituting them with more positive thoughts. He might be told to keep a journal and record all his negative thoughts about himself. This record would then be discussed in the next therapy session. In so doing some progress might be made in changing his habitual pattern of thinking, with beneficial result. Yet during this process no mention is made of his actual condition, his actual condition of being the source of his own well being.

What is being overlooked by the clinician in this case is calling attention to *the fact of thinking*, that it is not so much the *content* of the man's thoughts that is the problem – although they are certainly contributing factors – but rather that the man is unable to see how his awareness is senior to his thinking, and that by learning to recognize or see that *he is thinking* he can learn to find his real identity not in the thoughts – in which he believes without question – but in the *awareness* of those thoughts and feelings. By learning to find his real feeling of himself in his awareness he can also learn to question in a radical way the importance of a learned, conditioned habit of thinking about himself, a learned habit rooted in ignorance.

This latter approach, comporting well with spiritual teaching, promises to free the man from his ignorance, allowing him to experience more readily the always already available well being as reflected in a quieter mind. It also frees him from having to "work on himself" by challenging his thoughts, writing them down, and so on; instead, he is encouraged to become more interested in the natural, always available feelings of well being as reflected in a clear, intelligent mind.

Other psychological approaches invite clients to dreg up their past traumas, mistakes, and regrets, all as a way to "heal" them and restore their mental health. This usually unhelpful way to repairing the past only retraumatizes people with little resulting benefit. It too ignores the real help available and in fact even further veils the source of well being from view.

I hope you can see from these examples how easy it is to complicate what should be a simple, easy matter of reorienting people to their source of mental health. I also hope you can begin to see that the root of such mistaken attempts to improve mental health is grounded in a mistaken identity.

CHAPTER NINE

Identity

You have remained my companion in thought through some potentially difficult yet ultimately simple ideas concerning need, desire, object, subject, ignorance, knowledge, experience, and health. Throughout I have asked you to accept provisionally these ideas, to consider them as working hypotheses so that we might be able to continue this exploration together. Now the time has come to consider the most challenging idea of all: the notion of identity.

To be sure, I have discussed this idea with you before, in previous chapters, but now I want to explore it further because it touches the heart of the human experience and has also caused considerable perplexity among mental health practitioners.

If you will permit me to cite one example, I should like to mention the psychoanalyst Mark Epstein, a clinician who has written a number of books exploring how his treatment modalities have been influenced by his spiritual orientation, which happens to be Buddhism. Epstein writes that he is a faithful follower of Sigmund Freud, the initiator of psychoanalysis as a clinical practice intended to return disturbed individuals to a more well adusted life. Freud came to believe, based on his clinical experience, that the course of therapy should follow three stages: remembering, rehearsing or repeating, and working through. That is, a client or analysand should first remember an emotional impediment to health, then repeat it with the clinician, and finally work through it, eventually bringing the therapeutic process to some sort of conclusion.

What Epstein found in his own practice is that while the first two steps appeared to work well the final stage, working through, did not work well at all unless and until the client was able to *shift the feeling of identity* from the individual identity that felt deeply the emotional impediment to an *awareness of that identity*, from the usual feeling of self to a feeling of self or identity as awareness. Only by so doing was the client able to "work through" the impediment and attain some measure of healthy closure to the therapeutic process.

I have taken the chance of taxing your attention with this example in order to illustrate the necessity of a shift in identity even in more traditional modes of psychotherapeutic practice. In more healthy modes of practice such a procedure would not even be undertaken, as there is no need to remember or repeat and certainly not "work through" past emotional impediments to mental health. All that is needed is knowledge, a thorough reeducation regarding how the mind works and how ignorance has blinded us to this working.

Our real identity is awareness, but through ignorance we have taken our identity to be the *objects* of awareness, the thoughts, feelings, opinions, and beliefs that have been conditioned into us by parents, peers, teachers, and the holding culture. This false identity is then continually reinforced by every conceivable influence that surrounds us. We have little or no opportunity to question what we take for granted as being "ourselves."

What makes it even more difficult to free ourselves from this ignorance is that our psychic life, especially our thoughts, are in service to the process of desire, a largely unconscious process that operates out of our conscious minds. The baneful influence of this process is not so much that it distorts expressions of real need but that it binds our sense and feeling of identity to itself. So that it is not only that our thoughts and feelings are mistaken as our identity but it is also that our identity is captured and taken hostage by the process of desire. This process in turn makes it appear that our identity is at one with our usual motivations, which by and large are enslaved by the agitation of trying to sate an endless procession of desires.

It is this process of desire that makes it so hard to detect a reflection of our true nature even when a desire is sated for a time. We get a brief glimpse only to be overtaken again by yet another desire. Along with this is the mistaken belief that whatever happiness or satisfaction we *do* feel is due

23

to the object we have managed to acquire. Thus the mistaken sense and feeling of identity is secured for all time unless and until we are introduced to the knowledge that can begin to challenge the entire unhealthy process.

I have tried to introduce you to this knowledge in this short book. My hope is that it has at least opened your mind and heart to another possibility of life and living. I encourage you to question your received, conditioned sense of identity, to see yourself as unchanging, timeless, limitless awareness, the fulfillment of all your sense of limitation, incompleteness, privation, and lostness.

I invite you to come home to yourself, to see that every fine feeling you have ever felt is sourced in your own true nature, and that by simply turning your attention to your own awareness you will find that peace and happiness patiently awaiting your discovery.

PART TWO

Sources

CHAPTER TEN

Psychology

The first major school of psychology that can be considered a source for the teaching contained in this book is the behaviorist school. Over the course of the 20th century, and on into the 21st century, this school has grown to include more and more of the human being in its theoretical and therapeutic framework; in doing so, it has had to borrow some key ideas and methods from spiritual teachings.

The growth of the behaviorist school can be divided into three stages. The first stage involved a basic behavior modification model of psychotherapy, itself founded upon the theories of researchers such as Albert Bandura and B.F. Skinner. This form of therapy proved most effective in the treatment of phobias, gradually exposing fearful individuals to phobic situations and by so doing reduce and even extinguish phobic reactions. Theoretical foundations saw the human being as a stimulus-response organism, not taking into account other presumed features like the unconscious.

The second stage became known as the cognitive revolution, during which time theorists and practitioners like Albert Ellis called attention to the important role of thinking in the disturbance of human functioning. This form of therapy, combined with appropriately targeted medications, provided much needed help to individuals suffering from mood disorders like depression and anxiety. By including more features of the human experience the behaviorist practitioner was able to intervene successfully in a wider range of human challenges.

The third stage in the evolution of the behaviorist school was one in which not only even more human features were included but also an explicit borrowing or adaptation of spiritual ideas and methods were adopted by clinicians. This adoption was spurred on by two equally significant developments: one, the increasing participation of clinicians in their own spiritual journeys, and two, the increasing realization of the need for therapeutic methods that addressed effectively more recalcitrant forms of human dysfunction such as borderline personality disorder.

The two methods most familiar in spiritual circles that were adopted by the third stage of the behaviorist school were mindfulness and acceptance. Mindfulness in particular has become a popular way of addressing dysfunction, alerting clients in therapy that their minds are usually either dwelling on past events with all their trauma and regret or anxiously anticipating the future. Mental health and well being, these therapists teach, is to be found in the present moment, and the best way to train the mind to recognize its always already abidance in the present is to be "mindful." We are always in the present. Where else could we be? Mindfulness is simply recognizing that inescapable fact.

The practice of acceptance, also a part of spiritual paths, is taking what has been called a nonadversarial posture toward dysfunction. Rather than opposing the facts of the human problematic in a futile attempt to conquer them, therapists encourage clients to adopt a friendly attitude, accepting symptoms provisionally as a way of attaining some measure of freedom from them. Part of this modality involves creating a larger context for the therapeutic work, including the possibility of attaining a wider and so more inclusive feeling of identity for the client. The client is actually induced to adopt a therapist's perspective to his own dysfunction, to regard it as if it were someone else's situation. In so doing a subtle shift in identity can occur with correlative therapeutic benefit.

A second major school of psychology is the psychodynamic school. This school had its inception in the work of Sigmund Freud with his practice of psychoanalysis. As David Bakan has shown in his *Sigmund Freud and the Jewish Mystical Tradition*, from its inception the psychodynamic school was drawing upon a spiritual tradition for its ideas and methods. The practices of free association and dream analysis were already being practiced in esoteric Jewish communities. As what Freud called the royal road to the unconscious, dream analysis was replete in the Hebrew scriptures and subsequent Jewish life and thought.

The primary stages of Freudian psychoanalysis were remembering, repeating or rehearsing, and working through. A traumatic emotional event, say, is remembered, then it is repeated with the therapist, and finally it is worked through, issuing in a satisfactory closure. Freud recognized that this procedure may last long enough, taking one such remembrance at a time, to qualify as an "interminable" analysis.

It is the final stage, working through, that has proved most difficult for analyst and analysand alike. As in the case of the behaviorist school, it is those clinicians who have embarked upon a spiritual journey who have discovered a way to overcome these difficulties. And it is in pondering the question of identity, with the analyst's help, that enables the client or analysand to work through whatever emotional material stymies her usual sense of self or identity. The topic of investigation shifts from the *what* of the past experience to the *who*, the experiencer.

Once this shift in investigation is initiated by the analyst, the client is empowered to shift her own attention from the disabling emotional material to the question of her identity. Particularly in the case of a childhood trauma, the client can more readily understand that her current identity is quite different from her childhood identity, and that she has carried forward the past experience into the present without reflecting upon the significance of her own growth and development. In addition, the analyst can help the client question even her current sense of self. As in the behaviorist school, more current developments in the psychodynamic school encourage the client to consider the benefit of a wider context of thought and feeling, in particular a larger, more inclusive feeling of self, of identity. Spiritual teachings regarding a more authentic feeling of identity may also be adduced in this process.

A third school of psychology that has had a bearing on the teaching in this book is the transpersonal school. From its inception the transpersonal school has adapted spiritual teachings and methods in its therapeutic approach as well as its theoretical orientation. The main theoretician in its early stages was Ken Wilber, articulated in a series of books that matched stages of growth and development to modalities of therapeutic approach. Here the approach was inclusive, and a client at the ego stage of development should, according to Wilber and clinicians like Roger Walsh and Frances Vaughn, be treated with ego level therapeutic interventions. During this stage of treatment the client could be nudged into further developmental stages, after which more "transpersonal" modalities could be effectively introduced. Long before the mindfulness rage overtook the larger field of psychology, the transpersonal school and its clinicians were using methods like mindfulness to help clients become more aware not only of their dysfunction but also of their innate mental and emotional resources.

Yet another school of psychology that needs to be included has become known as the three principles school. This school's inception was inspired by a spiritual teacher named Sydney Banks. Initially two psychologists, Roger Mills and George Pransky, adopted Banks' principles of mind, consciousness, and thought into their practice. I have received formal training in this school's approach from clinicians like Keith Blevins and Dicken Bettinger. The strength of this school is in its emphasis on the innate and natural well being or mental health of every person, no matter how apparently maladjusted or disturbed. The school highlights the importance of a shift in a client's attention from the content of thought to the fact of thinking itself.

Once a client is able to make this shift in awareness, he is also able to use his feelings or mood state as a barometer or feedback mechanism to alert or inform him regarding the quality of his thought. If the feeling state is negative, his thought is negative; if the feeling state is warm or positive, his thought is positive. What is vital is to understand that thoughts create our unique, subjective perceptions of life, our personal reality. Acceptance of this fact is key: if we wish to be able to access our innate mental health, we must accept that our thoughts create our subjective outlook, and that empowerment comes when we find our identity not in our thoughts but in our *awareness* of those thoughts, or rather in our awareness or recognition of the fact of thinking.

Teachers in the three principles school explicitly credit a spiritual teaching for its founding and development, and also recognize the underlying unity of all authentic spiritual teachings. This underlying unity states that our innate identity and so well being is veiled by negative and disturbing thoughts, by an agitation of the mind, and that the cure for human dysfunction is a shift in awareness from the content of thought to the fact of thought, from thought content to awareness.

CHAPTER ELEVEN

Spirituality

Every authentic spiritual teaching could be considered as a source for the teaching in the first part of this book; however, I will explore the few that have had the greatest impact upon my life and thought.

The first teaching is the esoteric Christian tradition, particularly as presented in the *Philokalia*, a collection of writings from the Eastern Orthodox Christian school. There the importance, indeed the necessity, of attention in one's prayer life is taught. In Western Christianity it is especially the teaching of *lectio divina* as presented by Abbot Thomas Keating and his centering prayer movement within the Catholic Church as well as other Christian churches. The instruction to Christians in both Eastern and Western churches is to become aware of their soporific state of being as well as their unquestioned identity.

Implicit in this instruction is the distinction between need and desire. The word that these Christians use for desire is usually *passion*. Jesus instructed his disciples to take up their cross and in so doing deny themselves, to sacrifice themselves to a higher purpose and state of being. Passionate thoughts in particular are seen as impediments to this sacrificial way of life. This teaching does not turn away from the idea of suffering, not in a masochistic sense but as the price paid for attaining a closer union with God and his will. To sacrifice one's own "will" to the will of God requires a measure of suffering, and Christ on the cross remains the paradigmatic symbol. Yet for those willing to pay the price the beatitude of the Lord is promised.

Another spiritual tradition worth mentioning is Buddhism, in particular Tibetan Buddhism, which incorporates all three ways or *yanas*: Hinayana, or the lesser vehicle, Mahayana, or the greater vehicle, and Vajrayana, or the adamantine vehicle. The teaching of the Buddha, that life as it is lived in ignorance is suffering, that suffering is caused by desire, and that the way to be free of suffering is the eightfold path, forms the basis for all forms of Buddhist thought and practice. It was in the Buddhist teaching that I first learned the significance of desire and its baneful influence, how it is usually a distant and distorted expression of a real need and how it further reinforces a mistaken sense and feeling of self. I mention Tibetan Buddhism especially because I have studied with several Tibetan lamas whereas other forms of Buddhism I have only approached through reading.

Vedanta is an even more ancient spiritual teaching sourced in the Upanishads, systematized by Shankara in the 8th century CE, and taught in modern times by such sages as Ramana Maharshi, Nisargadatta Maharaj, Atmananda Krishnamenon, Swami Dayananda, Swami Chitmananda, and, in more recent times, James Swartz. Until his relatively recent death Swami Dayananda was the most authoritative teacher of Vedanta.

There are different schools of philosophy labeled Vedanta, but Vedanta as taught as a practical method of liberation is nondual. Hence the name Advaita Vedanta is redundant. Vedanta teaches that we are mistaken in who we think we are, that we are unborn, undying, timeless, changeless awareness; it teaches that awareness is the only reality, for to be real is to be without change. Individuals and the creation itself exist but are not real in the sense of being changeless; all existing beings and things change and so from the view of reality itself are not real. However, since all creation is the energy of awareness in manifest form, all beings and all manifestation are awareness and so, in that sense, are real. If mistakenly taken as independent entities, beings in form are not real though they exist; if correctly seen as awareness in manifest form, they are real even though they are subject to change. Existing beings and things depend upon awareness for their being; awareness does not depend upon them.

Vedanta teaches that since reality is nondual – since the only reality is awareness – then all experience is self experience: self as correctly understood. It teaches that we are ignorant of who we are – awareness or the self – and that because of that ignorance we suffer; we place our value on objects of experience, thinking that because we desire an object of some kind obtaining that object will bring lasting satisfaction. Because we do experience a temporary cessation of desire upon attaining a desired object, we mistakenly come to believe that the satisfaction resides in the object. Vedanta teaches that on the contrary when the desire is removed what we actually experience is the self in one or more of its discrete reflections like happiness, joy, peace, satisfaction, contentment, and so on.

Vedanta also teaches that the main obstacle to a more consistent experience of the self is the parade of thoughts, beliefs, opinions, and feelings in the mind that not only mistake the source of happiness in objects but that also reinforce a mistaken sense and feeling of self, of identity. We mistake our self for the conditioning of our acquired personality, and in so doing find our identity in a collection of *subtle* objects in the mind, primarily thoughts. So we need to acquire *discrimination*, and learn to discriminate between the real subject, ourselves, and objects, including more subtle objects like thoughts and feelings. Rather than finding our identity in subtle objects we find it in an awareness *of* those objects; we find it in awareness itself. *All* experiences are experiences of the self, for there is only the self, only awareness. But first one must learn to discriminate higher from lower experiences of the self.

In the teaching of Vedanta, *knowledge* is the only cure for ignorance. No experience or collection of experiences can do the job, for after an experience of the self – perhaps an epiphany of some sort – the ordinary state of mind returns and with it the ignorance of our true nature. That awareness is our true nature is known; it is declared openly in the oldest scriptures, the Uphanishads, that "you are That," that you, I, and all human beings are awareness, called *Brahman* or "the Vastness." What this means is that realization, as James Swartz puts it, is the "hard and fast knowledge" that I am awareness, timeless, whole, and complete. That is my real identity.

What does hard and fast mean? It means that the *vasanas* or tendencies that have heretofore been binding have been neutralized; that the desires which arise in the mind no longer have a decisive hold on me, that I am free to follow them or let them go. The knowledge that I am awareness may sound only intellectual, but Vedanta provides a central method for the assimilation of that knowledge leading to *moksha* or freedom: self-inquiry.

Self-inquiry is the method of *jnana yoga*. Other yogas, like *karma yoga*, are also followed as ways to prepare the mind for the teachings of Vedanta; however, I will confine my remarks to self-inquiry. Self-inquiry is not asking "who am I?" because the answer is already known: I am timeless, changeless, ordinary awareness. Rather, self-inquiry is applying the opposite thought to any thought or desire that arises in the mind that is born of ignorance; self-inquiry is the practical application of the knowledge that I am awareness. If a thought arises that I am incomplete, deficient, fragmented, and so on, I apply the opposite thought, the truth that I am complete, sufficient, and whole.

The practice of the various yogas recommended by Vedanta is for the purpose of preparing the mind for the more consistent recognition of discrete experiences of reflected awareness. These discrete experiences of joy, peace, contentment, happiness, satisfaction, higher energy, and so on, are made more possible as the mind is freed of the agitation caused by desire and quiets: the reflection of the self or awareness in the mind becomes clearer and more accessible when the mind is quiet, *sattvic*.

Thus in Vedanta there is both discovery and development: discovery of the truth of my true nature, and the development of the ability to receive more consistently those discrete experiences that help solidify the conviction that I am indeed That, timeless, changeless, complete, nondual, free awareness.

The last spiritual teaching I will consider is the Gurdjieff Work. I have participated for the past 30 years in organized group work in this tradition so it is this tradition with which I am most familiar and which has influenced me the most. Gurdjieff was an Armenian-Greek, raised in central Asia, who searched for and found a lost and very ancient teaching that predates all the known spiritual teachings today with the possible exception of Vedanta. He then reformulated the teaching for our modern world and brought it to the West, finally settling in France just outside Paris.

Gurdjieff taught that we have two natures, a lower one and a higher one; part of the lower we have acquired and is our conditioning, our personality; the other part of the lower is itself part of our essential nature, while the higher forms the other part of our essential nature, buried after many years of acquisition of a mistaken sense and feeling of self comprised of thoughts, beliefs, and feelings – even sensations of the body. These feelings, thoughts, beliefs, and sensations, however, are fleeting and perfunctory; they skim along the surface of our being and do not permit access to higher feelings or thoughts.

The above way of putting our two natures needs to be fleshed out a bit, however. Our essential nature is in both the higher and the lower "centers" or "brains": for purposes of simplification the lower centers are three: the intellectual, the emotional, and the moving-instinctual or body centers. The higher centers are the higher emotional and the higher intellectual. The acquired part of our being, our conditioning or personality, manifests in the functioning of the lower centers: the function of thinking for the intellectual center, the function of feeling for the emotional center, and the function of moving and sensation for the body or organic center. The two higher centers are the fully complete and changeless part of our individual being, and manifest primarily as spiritual energy. But in order for this energy to be received, there must be growth or development in the lower centers; in particular, the intellectual and the organic centers must be connected.

Thus there is a part of our essential nature that can evolve and develop into a higher state of being, one that can take its proper place in between our conditioning and our higher centers with their spiritual energy. Gurdjieff describes this process as an individual evolution of being, the growth of essence. This part of our essential nature can change.

He also taught that we are fragmented, that is, our lower nature is fragmented into the aforementioned three parts: the head or intellect, the heart or feeling, and the body or sensation. Each part or "center" has its own attention, each has its own interest, and each goes its own way without any connection with the other centers of intelligence in our lower nature. Because of this fragmentation we are unable to access the higher energy of our higher nature, the energy of awareness that is the formless substance of all manifested forms. Thus it is not so much thought itself that is the obstacle to a realization of our true nature as it is that our thought does not see its needed connection to the body and, through that, to the feeling. The attention mentioned in each center is the essence or the intelligence of that center. These attentions have the potential to become more active and attract the even higher attention or awareness of the higher centers because they are related to the higher in essence.

Students entering a house of work in the Gurdjieff school are given ideas to ponder but also various "forms" or activities that assist in assimilating the ideas into the tissues of the body. Chief among these is the practice of self-remembering, which involves a division of the attention between the subject and any object. Actually, however, the real object is also the subject. Thus subject and object blend into one entity of contemplation. Authentic self-remembering, then, is nondual; it is not a subject seeing an object; it is only seeing, only awareness. The object is the subject; the subject is the object.

Gurdjieff also taught that there are two movements of energy in the human frame: a movement of dispersion of energy and a movement of collection of energy, a movement away from and a movement toward the source. The movement of dispersion is a continual movement of attention toward the outside, which includes the more subtle objects of thought and feeling; the movement of collection is one that must be undertaken voluntarily; it involves struggle because it must be made conscious, and in so doing goes against all the soporific forces of nature and culture.

The Gurdjieff teaching maintains that ordinary awareness as manifested in the usual state of consciousness is not real consciousness in the human frame but is nearer to ordinary perception. In the human structure the lower centers must be brought closer together in order for real consciousness or awareness to manifest; the activity of attention connecting the mind with the body must be strong enough to receive spiritual energy from the higher emotional center. This state corresponds to the discrete experiences of self sought in the Vedanta teaching. Thus what this teaching about "real consciousness" in the human frame refers to is the *discrete experience* or *recognition* of consciousness. As said before, all experiences are experiences of the self, awareness, or consciousness, but without recognition awareness cannot function as consciousness *in the human frame*.

The teaching of Gurdjieff regarding fragmentation appears to contradict the Vedanta teaching about the wholeness and completeness of the real self. Gurdjieff, like other spiritual teachers, maintains that we begin with a need for being, and that this need reflects a real privation, an incompleteness in our being. But this privation is a lack on two levels of our manifested being: the lack of connection among our lower centers of intelligence, and a lack of being able to receive the higher influences needed to develop in the way that human beings are meant to develop. For just as we were meant to develop physically, cognitively, and emotionally, so we are meant to develop spiritually – this need for development is taught in all spiritual traditions.

The need for development does not apply to our true nature, that is, the higher part of our essential nature. Gurdjieff taught that our higher centers are already complete, whole, and fully functioning; the problem is that our lower centers, in their disconnection, are unable to receive the higher energy needed to develop an intermediate level of being, situated in between the lower and higher natures. And it is this development, according to Gurdjieff, that is meant to take place in the human frame in order for a given human being to occupy his intended place in the overall cosmic manifestation. Here I refer again to the previously discussed evolution of essence, of the lower part of our essential nature.

What is needed, then, is not only a more consistent reception of higher energy or discrete self-experiences but also a higher development intended to fulfill man's purpose for his existence. It is not enough to realize one's true nature; one must also develop sufficient being to take one's proper stand in the manifested order.

CHAPTER TWELVE

Philosophy

David Hume, a British philosopher in the tradition of empiricism, the notion that our knowledge comes to us through our experience, taught that our thought life is in service to our passions, our desires. He actually put the point more radically than that: he wrote that our thoughts are enslaved by our passions. We are deceived, he maintained, if we believe that our thoughts are free of the decisive domination of our desires.

In this portion of his philosophy Hume is very close to our spiritual traditions, which teach much the same doctrine. But whereas Hume was resigned to this fact, our spiritual traditions offer varied remedies for it, culminating in some form of an *experienced* freedom from desire.

The development of Western philosophy since Rene Descartes has been by and large a tussle between doctrines explaining how we come to know ourselves and the world about us. Along with this struggle of world views came a tension between certainty and change, between being and becoming. Some thinkers, following Plato and Plotinus, emphasized the need for certainty and being, while others, following the much later thinker Goethe, emphasized the need for change and becoming.

Immanuel Kant, awakened from what he called his dogmatic slumber by Hume, felt the need to establish once and for all certain knowledge about ourselves and the world. He believed that Newton had already accomplished that through his scientific achievements, but Hume had once again radicalized Western thought by calling into question the notion of causation – the idea that for every thing or event there is a cause. Hume maintained that real knowledge is derived from observation, and that no cause is ever observed; instead, what we observe is one thing or event following another. We add the notion of cause onto what is actually observed and then wrongly claim to have observed a cause-effect sequence.

This skepticism regarding our scientific knowledge was intolerable for Kant, yet he could not refute Hume's argument; in fact, he agreed with it. Yet, thought Kant, there must be some way to explain the certainty of Newton's theories.

Kant also felt distress about Hume's teaching that our will is enslaved by desire. He was quite sure this was wrong, but experience appeared to support it, given that the common run of man did seem to be dominated by passion. In effect, Kant also wanted certainty about our freedom to will the good, a freedom from the desires that dictated so much ordinary behavior.

Kant hit upon the idea that Hume was on the right track when he maintained that we add the concept of cause to what we actually observe. Kant thought he had found the certainty he was looking for by finding it in the structure of the mind. We "add" the concept of cause to our observations because that is the only way we can structure our experience, just as we must utilize the concepts of space and time to organize the chaos of impressions that would otherwise overwhelm us. Likewise we must have concepts such as subject and object in order to organize sense impressions like patches of color and formal shapes. The certainty we need is not to be found in objects but in the subject, in the structure of the mind.

Kant also taught that we have two natures, a lower nature and a higher nature. Here he found a way to overcome Hume's argument that our will and thought life is dominated by desire. Kant taught that this is true only for our lower nature; our higher nature is free of desire, and is thus capable of rising above personal interests or inclinations and following maxims that are not individual but categorical, applicable to all men and women of reason. In order to exercise our free will, in order to be free of desire, Kant said, one must act without any personal motive or inclination. In this way Kant believed he had rescued the freedom of the will from the clutches of desire.

Kant's contribution to Western thought has further implications. He taught that the tradition he was schooled in, the rationalist school of Descartes, Spinoza, and Leibniz, was a school of dogmatic metaphysics, as was the empirical teaching of Bacon, Hobbes, Locke, and Berkeley. All these philosophers, with the possible exception of Locke, felt comfortable in declaring what reality is; they were all traditional metaphysicians. It was Hume that was skeptical of these claims, writing that he was unable to be comfortable with Newton's claim that his science accurately described reality. Kant wrote that Newton was wrong in that claim, that his science did not describe reality but only what we construct by our minds out of the sense data that reality presents to us. Thus we can only know reality as it appears to us; we cannot know reality as it is in itself.

This development in philosophical thought had a huge impact upon subsequent philosophy. For Newton's science left no room for freedom of the will except for a rather desiccated idea of the sort of freedom compatible with determinism. Kant's philosophy made possible, not metaphysical knowledge, but metaphysical belief, beliefs in freedom of the will, morality, and God. Not knowing what reality is in itself, Kant wrote, we are able to believe in freedom, morality, and God without the overhead of claiming metaphysical knowledge, trying futilely to justify that knowledge with reasons and argument.

Schopenhauer took over this perspective and added the direct and special knowledge we have of our bodies from the inside, including our thoughts and feelings as well as sensations. For some reason Kant had overlooked entirely this special access to our inner reality. Schopenhauer wrote that our willed activity just *is* the movement of our bodies, for example my willing to reach for a glass of water just is my reaching, so my reaching is not caused by my willing; the two are the same action. From this special access Schopenhauer posited the "Will" as the fundamental force of reality. As Bryan Magee writes in his book on Schopenhauer's philosophy, following Kant's ideas Schopenhauer treats this idea about the "Will" as a metaphysical belief only, suggested by our intuition of the freedom of the will as an inner force. Schopenhauer was uncomfortable with the name "Will" and would have preferred to use the word *force*, but did not want his idea to be confused with Newton's use of the idea of force or energy. Schopenhauer's usage in turn led to Nietzsche's idea of the "will to power" as a metaphysical belief in a force that drives the cosmos and is primarily observable in human beings. By and large, however, Nietzsche thought of the will to power as a psychological hypothesis only.

Writing during roughly the same period in Germany, Johann Wolfgang von Goethe, Germany's greatest poet and one of the world's most significant and original thinkers, rejected the spiritual idea of man's two natures and indeed questioned the idea that man has a nature at all; instead, he found the "essence" of a given human being in that person's life and works, his character and his creations. Goethe became the fountainhead for the more modern idea of becoming as opposed to being, of change or development as opposed to certainty.

Many subsequent philosophers, for example Kierkegaard, Schopenhauer, and Hegel, tried to reconcile Kant and Goethe –all to no avail. For they cannot be reconciled in rational thought, though each has something essential to contribute to a more complete philosophy.

Enter the contributions of Eastern philosophy congruent with spiritual teachings. Schopenhauer, the first philosopher to become well acquainted with Eastern thought, felt that the solution to the opposition of Kant and Goethe somehow lay there, but did not understand that the solution could not be expressed philosophically, in words, though he tried valiantly to do so.

Eastern thought could not resign itself to the limited range of knowledge that Kant imposed; instead, it offered remedies to this apparent limitation through the teaching of nonduality. Spiritual teachings agreed with Kant about the need for certainty and the significance of being, yet also urged the necessity for change and development. Eastern thought maintained that only through a practical work, through a struggle between the two natures of man, could a given man or woman come to a resolution between certainty and change, being and becoming. It also agreed that the subject held the key to certainty and being, not because of the structure of the mind, as Kant held, but because there is no object: there is only subject. This is the principle of nonduality.

Reality, that is, is nondual; it is not even one, which implies two or more. It is "not-two," nondual. Reality is awareness and only awareness, and the apparent multiplicity of beings and forms is only manifested awareness. There is the certainty of being, but for man to experience this certainty he must develop or become, he must change, grow, or evolve into a fit receptacle for higher being, higher energy.

The only philosopher of note in Germany who did not attempt to reconcile Kant and Goethe was Friedrich Nietzsche. He was a classical philologist rather than an academic philosopher, and he followed Goethe in celebrating change and development rather than certainty and being.

Two philosophers of religion who should be mentioned as having influenced my thought are Jacob Needleman and David Applebaum. Together they authored a text called *Real Philosophy*, and in that book made the study of philosophy so much more applicable to everyday life than the vast majority of philosophical texts. In addition, both men have worked directly with men and women who in turn worked with Gurdjieff along spiritual lines. Because of that exposure their thought has been directed toward the practical and away from the more theoretical or academic. My own spiritual involvement has had a similar effect on my approach to philosophy.

I would certainly be remiss if I didn't mention my youthful philosophical mentor, Walter Kaufmann, the philosopher who more than any other brought clarity to the English speaking world regarding both Nietzsche and Goethe's influence upon subsequent Western thought. It was also he who alerted me to John Dewey's important book *A Theory of Valuation*, which highlighted the connection between need and value, and it was in Kaufmann's own youthful *Critique of Religion and Philosophy* that he explored what he called "ontological need," a sense of privation that can only be filled by a desire for being, a wish to love and create, a wish to be as God.

It is this one desire, this wish to be as God, this faithful reflection of a need for being, that both explains our call to authentic development and the certainty of the reality of our true nature. For the existence of an authentic need demonstrates the existence of an authentic subject of fulfillment.

CHAPTER THIRTEEN

Theology

Religious thought, Eastern and Western, can be considered either philosophy or theology, but discourse about God or "the gods" must certainly be considered theological. In my own development several theological thinkers have been influential.

St. Augustine, the great libertine turned theologian, maintained that God was found most directly in man's ability to be aware, that the spirit breathed into man by God was not reason or thought except in the highest senses of those words; rather, the spirit is the attention or awareness of all subtle and gross objects, objects which are really the subject in apparent manifestation.

St. Thomas Aquinas, the fulsome Catholic theologian, taught that God is that reality without which nothing would be able to be. He formulated five "proofs" for God's existence but his deeper thought could dispense with them all as superfluous in light of God's obvious being or reality. For God is the traditional designation, in religious language, for being itself, for the fact of being, the fact that there is anything at all rather than nothing. Even to attempt to imagine nothing is a trick of the mind; in order to imagine nothing there must be being and a mind that is.

In modern times the theologian that has had the greatest impact upon my thinking is Paul Tillich. Tillich taught that all the traditional Jewish and Christian stories and attributes of God are symbols; none are to be taken literally. God is not a being, Tillich maintained, God is being itself. The statement "God is being itself," Tillich wrote, is the only nonsymbolic statement one can make about God.

Thus God cannot be a being within the universe he created, able to be seated upon a throne somewhere in the heavens or able to oversee his creatures as a father looks after his children. All such biblical images are concessions to our limited, finite minds, symbolic ways of trying to imagine what a beneficent reality must be like. We think of it as being loving and caring, for example. But just because God cannot be a separate entity within creation does not mean being itself, reality itself, is not conscious, not aware. Indeed, Tillich also maintained, reality must be more conscious, more accepting and inclusive, than we can ever be. Every higher, finer feeling must, he taught, be grounded in reality itself, being itself. Being must be the source of all goodness, beauty, and liberation.

Eastern thought about God or the gods is usually considered philosophical, yet all talk about God or gods is also theological. Vedanta, for example, speaks about *Isvara*, the creator, which refers not to a god exactly but to the power of awareness to manifest itself in a created order. In the *Bhagavad Gita*, one of Vedanta's most sacred scriptures, an incarnation of God, Krishna, teaches Arjuna about reality and *karma yoga*, a form of yoga that prepares the mind to receive the energy of truth.

Buddhism abounds with *avatars*, bodhisattvas or buddhas who elect either to descend to us or remain with us in order to work for the enlightenment of all beings. Gautama Buddha claimed to be an ordinary human being who attained enlightenment, but subsequent Buddhist teachings elevated him to a godlike status in their pantheon. Tibetan Buddhism has a number of figures like Green Tara who offer help to men and women struggling for liberation, and exceptional practitioners like Guru Rinpoche continue to appear to and assist practitioners long after their own passage from this life into their next incarnation. My limited exposure to the Dawn Mountain Tibetan Buddhist Center and the teaching of Anne Klein has been most helpful in my spiritual journey.

Most Christians consider Jesus to be the one and only incarnation of God. He has two natures, and is fully human and fully divine. He is the second person of the triune God, but he is also the son of an earthly mother, Mary. Catholic teaching maintains that Mary herself was immaculately conceived in order to prevent her passing to Jesus the taint of original sin. Thus although Jesus is the son of Mary he is also the unblemished son of God.

The above scenario prepares the Christian mind to accept Jesus as the perfect sacrifice, pleasing to God. The model of this sacrificial atonement that has most influenced my own thinking is that of the Catholic church. In opposition to the teaching of the Reformed tradition of Luther and Calvin, the Catholic view is based upon the ancient Hebrew notion of sacrifice. There the Hebrews were commanded by God to bring their first fruits, their best lambs, for example, as a meritorious offering in repentance for their sins. In that setting God was not seen as venting his wrath upon the lamb offered; the lamb was not considered to be a substitute for the man offering it. Rather, God was pleased to forgive sin based upon the *teshuvah* or turning of the man's heart to God in repentance; God accepted the token of sacrifice as a meritorious, symbolic act.

In stark contrast to this meritorious offering perspective, the teaching of Luther and Calvin is that God vented his wrath upon Jesus, substituting a pure individual for a sinful one. This I consider to be turning the Christian God into an unjust tyrant, and is unbiblical to boot. Just as God did not vent his wrath upon an innocent lamb in the Hebrew Bible, so God did not vent his wrath upon his son. Instead, God accepted Christ's voluntary sacrifice as a meritorious offering for the sin of mankind, and for those who accept Christ's gift of love God grants the grace to live and love in like manner, as a meritorious sacrifice.

To better understand the monstrousness of the Reformed view, an analogy might help. Let's say I have offended my wife and I wish to express my regret and also wish to repent, never to do again whatever act displeased her. As a token of my regret and repentance, I bring her a bouquet of flowers. Following the Reformed view, the reaction of my wife would be to stomp on the flowers, venting her wrath on them instead of on me. But we all know that would not be her response. She would instead be pleased with this token of my remorse, place them in a vase as a reminder of my wish to renew my right relationship with her. Similarly, God is not eager to punish an innocent substitute like Jesus for my sin; rather, he accepts Christ's meritorious sacrifice and sees me as he sees Christ – provided I accept Christ's sacrifice as my salvation. I am grateful to and acknowledge Catholic theologian David Anders for this analogy.

Another theologian that has had considerable influence on my thinking is Alan Watts. His book *Myth and Ritual in Christianity* is a marvelous treatment of the Christian account of Christ's life as it is traced in the annual religious year. Watts' primary message is that Catholic dogma is a representation in symbolic form of an eternal truth. The incarnation, for example, is symbolic of the eternal truth of our two natures, human and divine. He is not saying that Jesus did not have two natures; he is saying that the Christian teaching of the *exclusive* two naturedness of Jesus is to read wrongly and literally a symbolic teaching about our embodied divinity.

Yet another influential theologian in my thinking is Abbot Thomas Keating, abbot of Snowmass monastery in Colorado. Keating is founder and principal director of Contemplative Outreach, a teaching ministry that endeavors to bring the sort of spirituality formerly confined to monastic enclaves to those who are not monastics. He teaches the levels of contemplative prayer through a method called centering prayer, and in so doing eases Christians away from an exclusive reliance on the spirituality of petitionary prayer toward the silent, contemplative prayer characteristic of monastics.

The esoteric and even exoteric Jewish tradition in its teaching about God has also exerted a decisive influence on my thinking. In particular, the more esoteric Jewish practices like *kavanah* direct attention both to God and to one's self, giving private and public worship a sacred dimension that is then, for practicing Jews, carried into ordinary life. My early teacher Walter Kaufmann did much to turn me toward Judaism. Jewish thinkers who have most influenced me include Martin Buber, Emil Fackenheim, and Richard Rubenstein. I use the word *thinker* rather than theologian because Buber would strongly reject the latter label.

In the effort to think and speak about God, and in the even more demanding effort to carry such ideas into ordinary life, theologians assist us, as the Jewish tradition says, in hallowing the everyday.

To round out this account of theological thinkers I should mention the relatively recent publication of Jacob Needleman's *What Is God?* This important and interesting work fleshes out Gurdjieff's "whim" to introduce a new conception of God to the world. I highly recommend its close and careful reading to any and all. Its subtlety is such that it defies any synopsis attempted here, although I can say that it explores the inextricability of higher awareness and higher energy.

CHAPTER FOURTEEN

Shakti

Shakti, or *prana*, is the spiritual energy of the manifested order; it is the formless substance that constitutes all form: physical, subtle or psychological, and spiritual. I consider it to be one of my "sources" because I have a personal relationship with it. It is the source both of my being and my becoming.

I should try to give an autobiographical account of this relationship in order to give you some idea of the importance of *Shakti* both to me and to spiritual aspirants in general. At the age of 44 I entered an organized spiritual school for the first time. I had been studying spirituality and religion in academic settings since my early 20s, and before that had brief encounters with Sufism in Turkey and Zen in Japan while serving in the military.

Upon entering an organized Gurdjieff group I devoured every related book on that tradition, and was very motivated to participate in the group activities despite my previous aversion to groups of any kind. After the first month of such participation I was in bed, somewhere between sleep and waking, when the top of my head opened and the most blissful energy imaginable entered the crown of my head and descended into my body. The same thing happened on a subsequent night. After that, during the day, I began to experience powerful headaches, especially in the back of my head and neck; it was as if an energy or substance wanted to descend but was blocked, prevented from doing so.

I was surprised and puzzled by these developments. I was beginning to attain an intellectual understanding of the Gurdjieff teaching, but was totally unprepared for what was happening to me. I was also hesitant to share these events with anyone in the group, so called my friend and mentor Kevin Langdon, at the time a 20 year member of the San Francisco Gurdjieff group and a student of John Pentland, the man Gurdjieff had appointed to lead groups in the United States. He normalized these experiences for me, saying that such things can happen upon entering a serious work group. I still felt somewhat at sea, however, because our group leader, Dick Brower, based in New York and also a pupil of John Pentland, had never explicitly talked about such things except for allusions to "higher energy" from time to time. After several weeks I decided to approach him about the matter.

He told me that "higher mind is trying to find a channel into your body; that's what's happening to you." I was relieved to find my experience normalized again, and after a couple of months working in group settings the energy did find its way down my back, ending the painful headaches. Before that occurred I had several experiences of the energy entering my head without passing further down the neck and back. At the time I was teaching at a university; one day, in the middle of a lecture a strong current of energy entered my crown and descended into my head. Fortunately I was able to continue the class without undue disorientation that could be noticed by the students. The same thing happened on another occasion when I was walking my dog.

Upon first entering the school of inner work I was told to sit or meditate every morning; this I did faithfully, never missing a sitting. After the *Shakti* had found its way down my back, whenever I took my sitting position on the pillow, the very instant my sitting position was assumed, the energy would descend. I needed no time to "allow" it or "open" to it; it just did so unbidden. This unbidden descent of energy also came as a great surprise.

At first the energy only descended; after several months I began to notice it ascending up the front of the body as well. The strongest sensation was at its terminal point in between the eyebrows, what some spiritual traditions refer to as the "third eye." I began to study the current of energy, and noticed a regular intensification, an ebb and flow, to it. It would regularly intensify, then ebb in its intensity, then intensify again. I then noticed that this ebb and flow was connected to the breath: upon exhalation, the energetic flow would intensify; upon inhalation, it would diminish slightly. This phenomenon reminded me of Gurdjieff's teaching about the active elements of air being a kind of food for what he called the "astral" or second body. I could actually feel this nourishment being deposited. It took some years later to discover where.

Twelve years into my participation with the group I discovered my center of gravity. To the best of my knowledge and memory this center had never been mentioned by any of our New York group leaders. At the time I was counseling emotionally disturbed individuals, and during one of my counseling sessions I felt the *Shakti* descend down my back and strongly deposit itself into my lower abdomen. I had felt it pass this area countless times, but had never felt it so strongly; it was as if it were saying "this is where I am destined to be; this is what attracts me." I was familiar with the Zen teaching about the *hara*, which has considerable importance in that tradition, but had never heard any Gurdjieff teachers speak about it. I knew, however, that I had made an important discovery for my inner development: I had discovered the wellspring, the source of my being and becoming, and the principal source of attraction for the *Shakti*.

I did not find any outside validation for my discovery until the publication of Jeanne de Salzmann's book *The Reality of Being* some ten years after I found my center of gravity. Jeanne de Salzmann was Gurdjieff's chief pupil, the leader of the Gurdjieff tradition world-wide after his death, and John Pentland's guide. In that book she refers to this center repeatedly, and even devotes one entire section of the book to its discovery. Long before that time, and certainly since that time, my development has been guided by the *Shakti*.

The *Shakti* is in effect the inner guru about which so many spiritual traditions speak; it is the energetic manifestation of the Master, the real Self; it is the energetic dimension of the reflected awareness in a still mind. It is the ultimate guide for an individual's spiritual journey to realization and to the mind's enlightenment. Realization is knowing that I am the light; bringing the mind along to be in agreement with that recognition is called enlightenment.

And yet there is another, important notion of enlightenment, one connected to the body and its reception of *Shakti*. Enlightenment, so this idea goes, is the flow of spiritual energy through the center of the body. For me, then, there are two, equally vital notions of enlightenment, one for the mind, the other for the body; the two notions come together as the body and mind join to receive spiritual energy or *Shakti*.

I have given you an account of my own spiritual journey so far. I can tell you that development continues after realization. It is a never ending process of allowing more and more of manifested awareness into one's life, of searching always for a place in between the higher world sourced in the Self and the lower world of physical and psychological manifestation. Now listen to the testimony of spiritual teachers across different cultures and traditions.

The 20th century sage Ramana Maharshi declares that
> The question arose in me, what is this I? I felt that it
> was a force or current existing in connection with the
> body . . . . The dormant *Shakti* manifests when the
> mind does not wander. The *sattvic* [quiet] mind
> resolves itself into the life-current. . . The *prana-*
> *Shakti* is the life-current. That peace is your
> natural state. It is called the current. That is your
> true nature.

The 20th century Tibetan lama Chogyam Trungpa taught that
> The goal of practice is to collect dispersed energies
> into the central channel, which corresponds to the
> experience of the innate Buddha-mind within.
> Through practice the *prana* [*Shakti*] can be brought
> into the central channel. Then the mind can recognize
> the fundamental nature.

Another Buddhist lama, Tenzin Wangyal, writes that
> The central channel is the channel of nonduality.
> It is in the central channel that the energy of
> primordial awareness moves. Wisdom *prana*
> moves in the central channel and is the energy of
> *rigpa* [awareness]. . . When the *prana* abides in the
> central channel one can abide in the nature of mind.
> The *prana* and the mind [meaning awareness in
> Buddhist teaching] always move together; there is
> no mind without *prana*.

From the Hindu tradition we have the testimony of 20th century teacher Sri Aurobindo:

> The Force gathers an ever denser strength and an independence. . . . This force has movements and it rises and descends within. It is not only a force but a presence. We have touched the fundamental reality of our being.

Sivaya Subramuniyaswami writes that a great soul

> sees himself as pure awareness. He says to himself, "I am pure energy. I am the spiritual energy that floods through mind and body." The meaning of *I* begins to change. *I* means energy, awareness. Just sit and be the energy in your spine and head.

According to Swami Chetananda

> As we begin to quiet our minds we become increasingly aware of the energy of life itself. Pure awareness is utterly still. At the same time, this conscious energy is dynamic. So pure awareness and conscious energy are completely interpenetrated. They are a simple reality. . . . It is not possible to have a real idea of what I am talking about until one has understood one's own nature as energy.

Yoga teacher T.K.V. Desikachar said that

> The flow of *prana* is the working of *purusha* [Self]. The *susumna* or central *nadi* [channel] is the ideal path for *prana*. The collection of *prana* in the body brings about inner peace and true understanding.

From the Gurdjieff tradition, Madame de Salzmann teaches that

> The flow of energies is the central thing in the Work. What is required? To quiet the mind, to have no tensions. The higher energy is the permanent Self.

> Everything in the Work is preparation for that
> connection [with higher energy].

And finally Adi Da Samraj writes that
> By surrendering into the Life-Current we may
> transcend all limiting associations with the phenomena
> of body and mind, and so regain our intuitive
> identification with the Radiant Life-Current or
> Transcendental Consciousness. The Transcendental
> Consciousness and Radiant Life-Current are realized
> to be One.

Enlightenment of the mind is the certain and undoubted conviction, the hard and fast knowledge, that I am awareness; the *experience* of enlightenment, what I wish to experience more and more, is, as Buddhist lama and teacher Anne Klein has written, "finally simply a matter of the inner winds [energy] coursing through the very center of the body." The experience of this energy is the highest manifestation of awareness or my true nature that I can allow into my life, and upon its reception and transmission my further development depends.

Shakti is at bottom awareness aware of itself in the human body. It is the movement of awareness through the body. Not the movement of our usual attention, the attention for which we have responsibility; rather, it is the reception of another attention or awareness altogether, a higher attention that can only be received when our lower centers of attention are connected and working together at a higher rate of vibration.

It would be a mistake to think of *Shakti* as just another subtle object of awareness like a thought or feeling. *Shakti*, like awareness, can never be an object; *Shakti*, like awareness, is the Subject. We are aware of *Shakti*, but not like we are aware of objects; we are aware of *Shakti* as we are aware of awareness. *Shakti* and awareness – *higher* awareness or attention – are just two words for the same reality. The testimony of the teachers and sages I have quoted above all decisively and authoritatively aver that *Shakti* and higher awareness are one.

What this means is that during the period that a given aspirant is learning to discriminate himself from subtle objects like thought it would be a serious mistake to take himself to be other than received spiritual energy, to see himself as awareness and *Shakti* as another subtle object. Spiritual energy is always, already, and only the Subject.

I have already alluded to a place "in between," in between the force that draws our attention outward toward objects and the force that draws our attention inward toward the subject. There is also a place "in between" in the body: the center of gravity, the *hara* or abdomen. This location in the body lies in between the descending force and the ascending force; it is the place that attracts the energy from above the head and from which the energy ascends to touch and open the *chakras* or energetic centers.

The search for a place in between leads to the discovery of this center, and the search for a place to rest and abide in this moment begins there. Countless energetic deposits in this place create an indestructible force; once tapped, a wellspring of living energetic water flows from the belly. The source of well being and Being itself, the source of the life current, invites our return to this place again and again.

CHAPTER FIFTEEN

Nonduality

Nonduality, the idea that reality is "not two," has formed the backdrop for all that has gone before; therefore, it should be fleshed out in more detail so that previous topics may be better understood.

Through the ages there have been spiritual and philosophical schools of thought that have been dualistic, that is, ways of conceiving reality that posit the ultimate nature of the subject-object division. But such schools have been theoretical in nature. When it comes to the actual practice of spiritual paths or forms, practitioners cutting across different traditions and cultures have always taught the nondual nature of reality. Whether it was Plotinus and Neoplatonism in the West, or Nagarjuna and Mahayana Buddhism in the East, nondual teachings have prevailed over the more theoretical arguments for duality. The reason is clear: the nondual perspective comes into view as one progresses along a given way or path of liberation.

As one begins a given way or path, the dualistic perspective is of course natural; after all, it is the perspective shared by virtually every individual in every culture. I am here, you are there; I am here, all objects are there. I am the bodymind, and as such every thing and every one separate from my bodymind is separate from me, is an object known to me. This perspective is a useful one from which to begin my journey into the unknown; indeed, it is the only perspective possible, unless I make the mistake of simply accepting the nondual teaching of a given sage intellectually. To do so would be a mistake because it would be a form of coercion, trying to force the mind to believe something that does not correspond to my experience. If nonduality is the truth, I need to be able to experience it for myself.

So I begin by taking myself to be the bodymind – or, to simplify a bit, by taking myself as the body. In taking myself to be the body, I naturally conceive reality from a dualistic point of view. The usefulness of this perspective is seen in a given teaching's demand that I begin to discriminate myself from objects in general. Obviously I will have no trouble in doing that with respect to physical objects, but what about subtle objects like thoughts or feelings? Such objects are taken to be myself; I routinely identify with all my thoughts and feelings, but spiritual teachings ask me to reconsider this mistaken sense and feeling of identity, to look upon these psychic phenomena as objects rather than as the subject, as me.

As I begin to discriminate myself from my psychology, from my personality or conditioning, I also begin to look deeper into my nature, discovering more essential elements of my being like silence and stillness, elements that are manifestations of an awareness that is senior to what I previously took to be myself. I am aware of a thought; that thought is therefore an object to me; I am aware of my body; my body is therefore an object to me. Neither my thought, my feeling, or my body is me, the subject. I am awareness, and phenomena like thought are objects.

Suddenly I become aware of the fact that I am not the body after all; I am not the bodymind. A new perspective begins to come into view: awareness is not a feature of my body; my body is a feature in awareness. In the dualistic perspective, awareness is a function of the bodymind. After learning to discriminate the bodymind as an object, however, awareness becomes known as senior to all objects, including the body.

I am not the body after all; I am awareness, which contains the body as it contains all objects. Having learned to discriminate myself from objects, I also learn to see myself as the subject only, as awareness. And if I am not the body how can I still see myself as here and you there? How can I see myself as here and a given object there? I am the awareness that includes, that comprehends, that knows, all objects. Having learned to *discriminate* myself from all objects, I now begin to see myself as *including* all objects.

If I see myself as here and you there, I am unconsciously identifying myself with my body. That is a natural perspective to take, even for one who has spent years in learning that the truth is quite otherwise. If I am awake to the reality of the situation, I see myself not as here and you or another object there, but me as inclusive of "here" and "there," of me as the awareness that comprises all in one act of seeing. That is not a "natural" perspective, for it runs counter to all cultural conditioning. Yet it is the truth.

The truth of nonduality has interesting implications. Every experience is experience of the self, of awareness. All experience is nondual. I do not have to try to engineer a nondual experience; it is always already the case. To be sure, I can be asleep to the condition of nonduality; I can continue to take the dream of duality as real, but that does not turn a nondual into a dual experience. Duality is a cultural superimposition, nothing more nor less. It is reinforced by language and is caused by taking ourselves to be the bodymind complex. We unconsciously impose duality upon a nondual reality. Yet through spiritual instruction and experience we can learn to recognize experience as it is, not as we mistakenly conceive it to be.

This is why the question of identity has formed such an important part of this book. So long as I identify myself with bodymind phenomena, so long will I be unable to recognize the true nature of my experience. If I am the bodymind, the body, I will always be a subject here separate from an object there. If, on the other hand, I am awareness, my reality includes all objects, and nothing is separate from me. In fact, everything *is* me. That is the truth of nonduality.

This truth will seem preposterous to those who insist on taking themselves to be the body or the bodymind. Those of a scientific bent, for example, who can only consider awareness to be a function of the bodymind, in effect an epiphenomenon, cannot accept the truth of nonduality. For them awareness is a product of the electrochemical functioning of the brain. In that case a given individual will always feel separate from whatever is not part of the bodymind. For such a person reality is a duality.

But examine your actual experience. Such careful examination is what spiritual teachings encourage. Your actual experience is one in which your awareness includes all phenomena, whether of the body, the mind, or physical objects like other people, who presumably also have bodies and minds. Your experience is not actually that of a body here and an object there; these are cultural conceptualizations that have been superimposed on experience. Your actual experience, if for example you just look around the room you are in, is completely inclusive; every phenomenon is appearing in your awareness, and without your awareness nothing could appear to you. If you remove every object, including your thoughts and feelings, your awareness would remain; if you remove your awareness, nothing would appear; there would be no subject and no objects whatsoever.

What this means is that since you are awareness every experience is an experience of yourself. I do not need to seek self-experience. I need to seek *discrete* experiences of myself like silence, stillness, and higher energy in order to bring deeper riches of myself into my ordinary life, but I do not need to seek experiences of myself because *every* experience is self-experience. Without awareness, without myself, no experience is possible, and every experience is an experience of awareness – is composed of awareness, made up of awareness, the very substance of which is awareness. And I am That.

I also need to seek discrete experiences like higher energy in order to prevent the ego, my ordinary sense of self, from coopting this knowledge, thereby fortifying itself rather than submitting to a higher force, a higher manifestation of reality. The undoubted conviction that I am awareness is for the mind; the undoubted reception of higher energy is for the body. It is possible to have one without the other; I myself experienced years of bodily enlightenment without the enlightenment of the mind; another individual may experience the enlightenment of the mind without bodily enlightenment. The latter individual is in danger of having his conviction coopted by the ego, the ordinary sense of being an embodied self. What is needed to counter that mistaken sense is another feeling of embodiment, the feeling of being embodied by an energetic Presence, an awareness that is received from above and deposited in the belly below. The Master, the guiding inner guru, is that received embodiment.

CHAPTER SIXTEEN

Conclusion

I begin with an unconscious identification with the body – "the body" meaning the bodymind complex that includes my thoughts, feelings, and sensations. Thus I take the perspective of duality as reality, or at least as reality appears to me: I am here, objects are there. From this perspective, then, I must begin my search for who I am. I begin with a wish to know myself, and, if possible, to bring more of myself into my experience.

I see that I have certain needs, some physical, some psychological or social, and some spiritual. I see also that I have been taught to accept without question those desires that appear to be faithful reflections of those needs. My search for who I am begins here, with a questioning of what I really need. In order to enter into this question I must also question the claim of a given desire to be an accurate expression of a given need. Is it true that a given desire will inevitably be a faithful expression of a given need, and that the fulfillment of the former will constitute the meeting of the latter?

I also find that certain significant teachings – psychological, philosophical, and spiritual – maintain that the process or operation of desire rules or directs my life and that I am unaware of its baneful influence. I believe that I am a free agent but in reality desire – the process of desire – enslaves me through an unconscious operation of identification wherein I identify myself, my being or identity, with certain objects of desire, in particular those objects that I associate with the body: my thoughts, feelings, and sensations. What I am ignorant of is the fact that these subtle or psychic objects are in service to desire – not just specific desires but the process of desire itself, the process of unconsciously identifying my very self with objects thought to be associated with the body.

Here is where my sense of value becomes confused. I value whatever I think is important, and I have been led to believe, by family and culture, that the body and its associated phenomena are me, and, if me, important. I value the body as myself. In questioning the claims of desire, however, I am slowly led to question my sense of value. For it becomes more and more apparent that most desires are not faithful reflections of need but instead reflect the unconscious operation of a process of identification, a result of a mistaken identity.

If I am fortunate I encounter teachings that question my notion of myself as a subject of experience. As I begin my search I take myself to be the body; that is my identity; that is how I conceive of myself as a subject. All other elements of my experience, everything not associated with the body, are objects. I, the subject, am separate from them, the objects. Through the slow assimilation of the teachings I begin to learn to discriminate subject from objects in a more realistic sense. I learn that the phenomena of experience associated with the body are also objects; they are not me but objects known to me. I begin to feel that I have been living in ignorance of myself, that I am missing some essential knowledge about who I am.

The question of value is again introduced when I begin to wonder if I have been placing undue importance upon objects as the source of my well being. My family and culture have taught me to value objects as the source of my fulfillment, so of course it is natural for me to desire them. But the teachings I have encountered maintain that on the contrary lasting satisfaction comes not from objects but from the subject. I, the subject, am the real source of fulfillment. If this is so, what I should be desiring is myself. I wish to know myself, this self that is supposed to be the source of my well being.

I have the undeniable experience of fulfillment when I obtain an object that I have desired. Is the sense of satisfaction really in the object, or is it in myself? If in the object, why does the object that satisfies me not satisfy other people? Some objects, of course, may satisfy almost everyone, but other objects do not, and this fact makes me wonder about just what is making me feel good when I get what I desire. Here the teachings run counter to the culture: they maintain that when a desired object is obtained the desire

Gary Bryant

is removed and I experience the deeper springs of well being that is my self. But since I have been led to believe that the source of my satisfaction is in the object, I overlook the significance of this good feeling and, when it inevitably fades, begin looking for yet another object so that the feeling may be restored. Thus the process of desire and the mistaken valuation of objects form a formidable bondage over my will and my experience of life.

I am told that I am ignorant, that I ignore the reality of my being and so overlook what is really happening in my experience of dissatisfaction and satisfaction alike. Since dissatisfaction is in fact a recurring phenomenon in my life, I accept provisionally the idea that I am ignorant and that what I need above all is knowledge, a deeper knowledge of myself, of who I am. Am I really the source of fulfillment, satisfaction? I really need to know, for if true I have the possibility of breaking the bonds of the desire for objects and resting in the true source of well being. To begin to approach this question I need a combination of knowledge and directed experience.

The knowledge I obtain from the teachings; I need to be taught. I need to be told who I am, and the teachings reveal that I am awareness. I am not who I have taken myself to be all during the years of growing up physically, mentally, and emotionally. I am not my thoughts, emotions, and sensations. In brief, I am not the body. The body, my thoughts, emotions, and sensations, are objects known to me, just as I know another person or a physical object. I am the awareness of those objects, the awareness of the body.

Now that I have been taught I need discrete experiences of who I am, experiences that reveal my deeper reality and that assist in the assimilation of revealed knowledge. A school of self-knowledge is needed to facilitate this process, to obtain directed experience from those who know and to derive support from others similarly engaged in learning who they are. Spiritual exercises are given to help me experience myself as awareness, to help me discriminate my self from those objects that heretofore have been taken as my self. In addition, I need to experience those discrete features of the self that constitute the source of well being, features like peace, joy, love, contentment, and blissful states full of higher, spiritual energy.

As these helpful experiences accumulate I begin to sense and feel, deeper and deeper, more and more, another life in me that wishes to manifest in my ordinary life. I come to sense that my search is for a place in between the life I usually live and the deepening other life that is a manifestation of the source of well being. I recognize, more and more, that not only my mental health but also my identity resides in that source.

I also come to recognize that what I have been taught about this identity, this awareness, does not remove the mystery of who I am but rather deepens it, that who I am remains an unknown, and that just because I can now attach a verbal label like awareness to it does not make it an object to be known by a subject. Awareness cannot be an object; it is the Subject. I cannot know who I am in the conventional sense of knowing. I can "know" only by being what I am.

I can only experience awareness as it is reflected in a quiet mind. This experience is most important in assimilating the knowledge given me in a school of inner work. For in the continuing work of challenging my conventional identification with the body and my discriminating the Subject from all objects, I come to understand that what I initially separated from myself must eventually be taken back into myself. I am led, step by step, to experience myself as all and everything.

Discrimination must continue, however. My body, my thoughts, emotions, and sensations, are me, but I am not the body. My experience is me, but I am not my experience. All objects are me, but I am not those objects. These truths come slowly but surely. My true identity includes but also transcends experience and the objects of experience. So I say again: my experience is me, but I am not my experience. Perhaps a clearer way to say this is: I am my experience, but I am not *only* that. My Being, *I*, transcends my experience, so I am free from my experience. It is therefore incorrect to say, and most unfortunate to believe, that I am just my experience. My experience is me, but I am not my experience.

Eventually the question of what spiritual traditions have called realization or enlightenment may arise for consideration. Moments of realization come whenever we are awake to the reality of our being, whenever we are aware of our awareness. Such realization includes the discrete experience of embodiment, of feeling a presence – myself – in the body as higher energy, a higher substance that is felt as 'I.' But since the nature of experience is change, no limited experience or collection of limited experiences can produce a limitless result. Limitlessness is what I am; it is not a result of experience.

Experience can validate knowledge, but it cannot remove ignorance – only knowledge can. When ignorance is removed by knowledge, the light is revealed. Enlightenment is revealed light, the removal of ignorance, the firm conviction, the hard and fast knowledge, that I am limitless awareness. Enlightenment, the light, neutralizes the process of desire. Enlightenment is for the mind, and the purpose of self-inquiry is to educate the mind regarding reality. Enlightenment is for the mind, not for me.

Or perhaps a better way to put it is: enlightenment is for my mind; my mind is me, but I am not my mind. I am not enlightened; I am the light.

Similarly, enlightenment is for the body. Enlightenment in this sense is the undoubted reception of spiritual energy flowing through the center of the body. Here again, enlightenment is for the body, and while the body is me, I am not the body. I am the light, the *Shakti*, that courses through the body. As in mental enlightenment, I am not bodily enlightenment; I am the light.

Once these discoveries are made, further development awaits me. Not the 'I' that I am, but the me that I am, the me that changes, not the changeless 'I.' There is an essential form of being in me that can grow, can develop, through the reception of higher energy. Just as I developed physically, mentally, and emotionally, so I am called to develop a higher level of embodied being, in between the lower, acquired level and the higher, changeless level. This intermediate level is destined to remain in touch with both lower and higher levels of being simultaneously, to allow the passage of higher energy into the bodymind complex. In so doing I not only have a more consistent access to mental health and well being but also take my proper place in a living cosmos of interpenetrating energies.

Psychologist Abraham Maslow wrote about a psychology that would be centered not in man but in the cosmos. Authentic spiritual teachings have always been so centered. I begin my search for well being with questions of need, value, and identity, and end with a paradoxical combination of certainty and a greater recognition of mystery, of the unknown. I see that there is no ultimate conflict between being and becoming, between discovery and development, between certainty and mystery. I am certain of my identity, and certain that both certainty and mystery lie beyond the conceptual mind, beyond words, beyond the isolated, disconnected intellect. My being is Being itself, a reality that includes and transcends my embodied state of being. And that for the sake of the whole, for the sake of the cosmos, for the sake of all of manifested awareness, I must occupy my proper place as a receiver and transmitter of cosmic influences.

Thus our well being – yours and mine – is not for our sake alone. In the Tibetan Buddhist tradition all practice begins with dedicating the fruit of such practice to the benefit of all beings. May all beings benefit from your effort to realize and experience your innate well being.

Coda

Enlightenment is light received
Insight for the mind
Energy for the body
The place in between
Is a bodily location
Between the movement toward objects
And the movement toward the subject
Between the descending force from above
And the ascending force from below
The place in between
Is the source of growth and being
Welling up as rivers of living water
Arising from the belly
An oasis of life
Creates green pastures of rest and abidance
Attracting further nourishment
From above
Nurturing further growth
From below
A blossoming center
Of radiant life

Bibliography

Most source material for this book can be found in my trilogy: *Invicti Solis*, *The Liberation of Thought*, and *The Sickness of Effort*. This bibliography is intended for further reading for those so interested.

Applebaum, David. *The Vision of Kant*. Element. Rockport, 1995.

Bryant, Gary. *Invicti Solis*. Balboa. Bloomington, 2015.

_____. *The Liberation of Thought*. Balboa. Bloomington, 2015.

_____. *The Sickness of Effort*. Balboa. Bloomington, 2016.

_____. *Role Playing*. Balboa. Bloomington, 2017.

Buber, Martin. *The Eclipse of God*. Humanities. New Jersey, 1952.

Epstein, Mark. *Going to Pieces without Falling Apart*. Broadway. NY, 1998.

Kaufmann, Walter. *Critique of Religion and Philosophy*. Harper. NY, 1958.

_____. *Discovering the Mind*. McGraw-Hill. NY, 1980.

_____. *Without Guilt and Justice*. Wyden. NY, 1973.

Keating, Thomas. *Open Mind, Open Heart*. Amity. NY, 1986.

Klein, Anne Carolyn. *Meeting the Great Bliss Queen*. Beacon. Boston, 1995.

Magee, Bryan. *The Philosophy of Schopenhauer*. Clarendon. Oxford, 1983.

McGrath, Alister. *Christian Theology*. Blackwell. Malden, 1993.

Mindfullness and Acceptance. Ed by S. Hayes, V. Follette and M. Lineham. Guilford. NY, 2004.

Needleman, Jacob. *What is God?* Penguin. NY, 2009.

Norbu, Namkhai. *The Mirror*. Barrytown. NY, 1996.

Ouspensky, P.D. *In Search of the Miraculous*. Harvest. NY, 1977.

Philokalia. Trans. G.E.H. Palmer, Philip Sherrard, Kalistos Ware. Faber. London, 1984.

Pransky, George. *The Renaissance of Psychology*. Sulzburger & Graham. NY, 1998.

Ray, Reginald. *Secret of the Vajra World*. Shambhala. Boston, 2001.

Real Philosophy. Ed by Jacob Needleman & David Applebaum. Arkana. London, 1990.

Salzmann de, Jeanne. *The Reality of Being*. Shambhala. Boston, 2010.

Swartz, James. *How to Attain Enlightenment*. Sentient. Boulder, 2009.

Subramuniyaswami, Sivaya. *Merging with Shiva*. Himalayan Academy. India, 1999.

Talks with Ramana Maharshi. Inner Directions. Carlsbad, 2000.

Trungpa, Chogyam. *Cutting Through Spiritual Materialism*. Shambhala. Boulder, 1973.

Waite, Dennis. *Back to the Truth*. Mantra. Washington, 2012.

Wangyal, Tenzin. *Healing with Form, Energy, and Light*. Snow Lion. Boulder, 2002.

Watts, Alan. *Myth and Ritual in Christianity*. Beacon. Boston, 1968.

About The Author

Gary Bryant is an ordained priest in the Orthodox Catholic Church, a hospice chaplain with experience and education in business, psychology, philosophy, theology, religious studies, library science, addictions counseling, and hospital chaplaincy. He has investigated the subject of well being for over fifty years with thirty years experience in an organized spiritual school.

Gary is past President and the first Treasurer of the Prometheus Society, former membership officer of the Triple Nine Society, former associate member of the International Society for Philosophical Enquiry (ISPE), former member of Intertel, former lifetime member of Mensa, and a current member of the on line Four Sigma Society.

He enjoys participating in athletic activities with his wife, with whom he resides in the Houston metro area.

Gary is currently organizing a group interested in exploring further the topic of well being. Those desiring to participate in the group may contact Gary through Balboa Press or on his facebook page.

Printed in the United States
By Bookmasters